The Call

OBJECTS TALK BACK

About This Book Series

In collaboration with the Ethnologisches Museum and the Museum für Asiatische Kunst of the Staatliche Museen zu Berlin, the Stiftung Humboldt Forum im Berliner Schloss invited the writer Priya Basil to curate a series of events and books: *Objects Talk Back*.

Every year, Priya Basil asks two writers to engage with an object of their choice—either from the exhibited collection or from the museums' storage depots.

The project represents a new curatorial practice (complementing ongoing provenance research) characterized by transparency and dialogue regarding the collections in the Humboldt Forum, the complex history of its location and entanglements with contemporary global issues. The aim is to investigate the provenance history of the objects while simultaneously engaging in a direct dialogue with people biographically connected to the countries of origin, thereby fostering international multivocality and transforming museum practices.

Rawi Hage

The Call

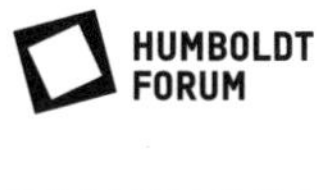

DIAPHANES

Double folio of a Manichaean book, recto, III-200
Languages: Old Turkic/Old Uyghur, Sogdian, Middle Iranian, Parthian
Scripts: Sogdian, Manichaean and Runic
Paper, ink
Ruin K, Kocho (Gaochang), Xinjiang, China
9th–10th century
16.4 × 21.4 cm
Museum für Asiatische Kunst – Staatliche Museen zu Berlin

The double folio belongs to a rare collection of Manichaean fragments discovered in "Ruin K" at Kocho, once an important city in the eastern Tarim Basin. The excavations took place at the beginning of the 20th century as part of the German Turfan expeditions, during which numerous artworks and manuscripts were collected in Kocho and Bezeklik and other sites in the Turfan region and then taken to Berlin.
The manuscript fragments are held in the Museum für Asiatische Kunst and in the Berlin-Brandenburg Academy of Sciences, and for over 100 years they have served as a major basis for research. The double-folio fragment contains texts in several languages and scripts, written in black and red ink. It vividly illustrates the cultural and linguistic diversity of the region.

OBJECTS TALK BACK

Objects have voices, which we may not hear. Literature helps us to listen.

Objects Talk Back is a project that asks: what are the possibilities of literature to open up new stories, questions and relations when writers engage with museum archives?

While there are promising currents of change, ethnological museum collections remain tied to violent colonial histories and ongoing practices of domination. Information for most objects is still limited to date of creation or acquisition, place of origin, type of material, collector or donator. Even these details are not always accurate.

The archaeologist Dan Hicks proposes "necrography," a practice of digging into the past to trace the colonial story behind an object.[1] Such an approach may reveal much of value, but also leave one "straining against the limits of the archive," as literary scholar Saidiya Hartman writes.[2]

Colonial archives contain their own prejudices and distortions. Hartman suggests "critical fabulation"—melding history, theory and fiction—"to displace the received or authorized account." Inspired by these ideas, I coined the term "fabulography" for *Objects Talk Back*. In a piece for *British Art Studies*, I describe fabulography as an invitation to work creatively with-from-through gaps, facts and imagination to expand the narrative space around an object.[3] Fabulography involves digging deep, uncovering painful details, but also rising up, celebrating, honoring, reconnecting.

Since 2021, two writers are invited each year to explore collections of the Ethnologisches Museum and the Museum für Asiatische Kunst, both part of the Staatliche Museen zu Berlin. The writers encounter objects displayed in the Humboldt Forum, Berlin, and also those stored in the museums' depots. They select an object, and respond however they wish—through fiction, poetry, narrative nonfiction, multimedia texts. Later, they present the finished work at a live event in the Humboldt

Forum. Now, objects talk back in a book series as well, affirming Hartman's appeal "to consider stories as a form of compensation, perhaps the only kind we will ever receive."[4]

Priya Basil

1 Dan Hicks, "Necrography: Death-Writing in the Colonial Museum," *British Art Studies*, Issue 19, 2021: https://doi.org/10.17658/issn.2058-5462/issue-19/conversation. | **2** Saidiya Hartman, "Venus in Two Acts," *Small Axe* (Indiana University) 12, no. 2 (2008): https://muse.jhu.edu/search?action=browse&limit=publisher_id:3 (accessed March 9, 2024). | **3** Priya Basil, "Writing to Life," *British Art Studies*, Issue 19, 2021: https://www.britishartstudies.ac.uk/issues/issue-index/issue-19/death-writing-in-the-colonial-museums (accessed March 9, 2024). | **4** Hartman, "Venus in Two Acts."

Priya Basil

Introduction

"Is there an autonomous republic of art that has survived across time and through many places? Do objects have autonomy?"[1] It was with such questions that writer and photographer Rawi Hage began his encounter with objects exhibited in the Humboldt Forum. More questions opened up as he spent time in the collections of the Museum für Asiatische Kunst with his partner, fellow writer Madeleine Thien. Accompanied by curator Lilla Russell-Smith, both authors were drawn to objects which came to Berlin via collections from the Turfan expeditions (1902–1914), from the region of the Northern Silk Road (present-day Xinjiang Uyghur Autonomous Region).

Rawi Hage was born in 1964 not far from Byblos, Lebanon, and grew up in Beirut. He lived through the Lebanese Civil War of the 1970s and 1980s and ended up in exile in New York for some years before migrating to Montreal, Canada, in 1992. In all of Hage's books, Beirut is a recurring presence, a character, an archive in itself: "everybody loves Beirut, everybody is scared of Beirut,"[2] he has written. At this site of so much disaster, so much wonder, he is compelled again and again to consider "the longer-term loss, a loss of what is deeper, of what matters, and what otherwise had the potential of lasting"—what, in his words, is "a world heritage, an intersection of religious, linguistic and cultural heritage. [...] A place once a refuge for every exile in the region."[3] His fiction evokes that place with love, sorrow, anger, sensuality and gorgeous doses of irreverence. As one of his characters remarks: "Laughter should be permissible under all circumstances."[4]

At the Humboldt Forum, Hage was drawn to a Manichaean manuscript written in two colors and two languages, Uyghur and Old Turkic: "I have chosen a fragment, a trace of a lost book, to explore the notion of residue, incompletion, imperfection, excavation; in short, what is lost and what little remains."[5] For her text, Thien selected the fragment of a wall painting of three Uyghur princes, donors who contributed to the construction of a grotto in the Bezeklik Thousand Buddha Caves. Both said they sought to examine the contained universes of transitory objects. Rather than thinking of histories as something to be controlled or possessed, they invite us to observe the movement, uprooting, displacement, migration, resettlement and flight of objects, within the context of conflicting yet organically connected beliefs. Amid all the flux, they found a continuity, which, in presenting their texts for *Objects Talk Back*, became the title of their joint event: "Fragments."

The Manichaean manuscript holds verses of poetry, including some that would have been chanted in prayer or during funeral ceremonies. "What remains in our hands today is a prayer for the dead," Hage reflects, "a sort of a requiem to itself, a chanting troubadour displaced from its original home, resurfacing to tell its own history." Hage's text shows how history is also always connected to, and inflected by, the one who narrates. The Manichaean fragment brought back his own past: "I was struck by memories of incantations I'd heard at the many funerals in the Eastern churches of Beirut, where I grew up. The church of my childhood conducted its ceremonial prayers and liturgy in two languages." He says, "During the years of the Lebanese Civil War, my family and I experienced a high frequency of deaths. The many funerals we attended inevitably inscribed these prayers in my memory, and these chants of death still occasionally resurface in my mind to this day."[6]

Hage, a fiercely secular thinker, has long been fascinated by religion. "There is no God, there are only humans who imagine the possibility of Gods,"[7] he writes in *Beirut Hellfire Society*. All his fiction probes the boundaries of the sacred and profane with a deep sense of death as finality. "Man's laws are self-serving, nature's laws are arbitrary, and God's laws are in need of some serious updates,"[8] he writes in *Carnival*. Yet Hage remains intrigued by Manichaeism, especially its creation story, which culminates in confrontation, destruction and a great scattering of light. "In the Manichaean belief system," he writes, "each of us contains these splinters of light. The only way for us to return to our original home is through knowledge."[9] But what exactly is the nature of this light, this knowledge? For *Objects Talk Back*, Hage turns these questions over and over, finding affinities between the Manichaean notion of dispersed light and the fates of displaced people and objects.

"The end can only be witnessed by those who persevere, the quiet survivors,"[10] Hage writes in *Beirut Hellfire Society*. His stories are full of survivors who share their tales. The manuscript, too, is one such survivor, inspiring Hage to connect the fragmented residues of Manichaeism with the fractured state of Lebanon, which he describes as "a microcosm of that encounter between East and West. There was always this mixture of religions. [...] For the most part, it was problematic, but there was also a period of grace, where coexistence happened."[11] This possibility of coexistence continues to intrigue him.

Rawi Hage has published five works of fiction, all of which have been nominated for Canada's most prestigious literary awards. His first novel, *De Niro's Game*, was internationally acclaimed and won many prizes, including the IMPAC Dublin Literary Award. He was awarded the Hugh MacLennan Prize for Fiction for his novels *Cockroach* and *Carnival*. He has received many stipends and fellowships, including at the DAAD in Berlin. More recently, his entire body of work was honored with the Writers' Trust Engel/Findley Award. His books have been translated into thirty languages.

In *The Call*, Hage's text for *Objects Talk Back*, we learn that, "For nearly a hundred years in the ninth century, Manichaeism was the state religion of the Uyghur Kingdom in the Turfan region. Sometime in the fourteenth century, however, in the wake of various wars and persecutions, Manichaeism disappeared. Its scriptures are preserved in a fragmentary nature, in different languages."

Different languages are present within Hage's essay too: it is accompanied by footnotes recording his rich email exchange with curator Lilla Russell-Smith. Their distinct voices and areas of knowledge echo the polyphony that characterized Manichaeism. I was copied on their professional correspondence, a witness to the generosity each showed toward the other's expertise. "I wish I could be a writer sometimes too, an artist, but my job is to be pedantic," Russell-Smith wrote to Hage. "[T]hese questions are so complex, and art and scientific research so different. [...] As always I am stuck between two worlds." For Hage, literature is "the space of ultimate freedom."[12] He took the space he needed and created a space capable of holding much more.

"The experience of encounter always remakes us,"[13] Hage and Thien reflected after their work for *Objects Talk Back*. In the most profound encounters, the sense of transformation is mutual. "I have also been changed in the process," Russell-Smith said. "Somehow meeting you both and reading your book sharpened my own focus and has helped me to plan my work for the next years." She intends to center her future work around fragments.

Hage traces the trajectory of Manichaeism, the lost religion, with melancholy, aware of the continuum of violence behind such erasures, the impossibility of retrieval, the challenges of restitution, of redress. Yet, as in all his writing, he dares to wonder about sparks of light amid the darkness, the fragile promise that may lie in syncretic coexistence: "Was the intention of the Manichaean gods and their light to be cut and fragmented, thrown into this world, dispersed and mixed? To be imperfectly seen yet known by both ignorance and knowledge, so that they could be reborn again and thus remain?"[14]

1 Email from Rawi Hage to the author, August 18, 2023. | **2** Rawi Hage, *Beirut Hellfire Society* (Toronto: Alfred A. Knopf Canada, 2018), p. 45. | **3** Rawi Hage, "In Beirut, a Nightmare Comes to Life," *Globe and Mail* (August 6, 2020). | **4** Hage, *Beirut Hellfire Society*, p. 100. | **5** Email from Rawi Hage to the author, August 23, 2023. | **6** All quotes in this paragraph from Hage, *The Call.* | **7** Hage, *Beirut Hellfire Society*, p. 226. | **8** Rawi Hage, *Carnival* (Toronto: House of Anansi Canada, 2012), p. 31. | **9** Hage, *The Call.* | **10** Hage, *Beirut Hellfire Society*,

p. 171. | **11** Interview with Rawi Hage by Matthew Hays, "Montreal Author Rawi Hage on His Wild-Ride Short Story Collection *Stray Dogs*," *Cult MTL* (April 1, 2022). | **12** "Rawi Hage on the Reasons Writing Is a Form of Personal Freedom," CBC online (May 16, 2019). | **13** Rawi Hage, email to the author, August 18, 2023. | **14** Hage, *The Call.*

Rawi Hage

The Call

We are here to reflect on the possibility of "speaking back to" a historical injustice committed by empires, various invaders and economic powers. Undeniably, the illegal acquisition of historical objects is a form of displacement of a people's sacred dignity and traditions. These injustices are the extension of sequences of savageries we humans have committed against each other, and still do.

The topic for me and for many of us is emotional. One must acknowledge that colonialism's brutality was systematic in its organization, know-how, acquisitions of knowledge, technological efficiencies and, ultimately, thefts.

I would like to acknowledge the tremendous expertise of Lilla Russell-Smith, Curator of Central Asian Art, Museum für Asiatische Kunst of the Staatliche Museen zu Berlin, in providing crucial research material on the chosen objects and conversing generously on many complex questions.

After immersing myself in many readings on the topic of restitution and its histories, I have decided not to approach this text, and consequently the Humboldt Forum, as a series of floggings and apologies. I have decided not to retread the path of one-directional condemnation, however pleasurable that might be. By avoiding a Manichaean tone, while nevertheless forcing you to embark on the topic of Manichaeism, I'm hoping to create a space for the object itself to manifest its own dialogue and erudition.

ITEM III-200

My object is what I would describe as the "fragmented leaves" of a Manichaean scripture. The words written on the leaves, or pages, are linguistically mixed, multifaceted and, I would add, multicolored. Officially, it is referred to in the system of the Museum für Asiatische Kunst as Item III-200. According to Professor Berker Keskìn, a professor in the Department of Old Turkic Languages at Istanbul University, Item III-200 consists of three parts. In an email to Lilla Russell-Smith, Professor Keskìn writes,

> I am also grateful for [this] precious fragment. There are three Manichaean Old Uyghur poems in this fragment. It is also noteworthy that the poems are titled in red ink.
>
> The first poem (recto, top left) is a hymn to the *taŋ t(ä)ŋri* (=Sogd. *vam vagı*). This poem is quite harmonious and gives the impression that it was recited during worship services. The verses are indicated with red dots. In the 14th and 15th verses ... the Sogdian number five [is written]. It refers to ... two verses [which] should be repeated five times.
>
> The second poem is just below the first. This relatively short poem is a prayer.
>
> The third poem, which bears [the title] "a different Turkish poem" ... begins below the second one and continues on the verso side. This rather long poem is a description of death. The poem is rich in rhyme

> and repeated [refrain]. The fact that it is harmonic [in cadence] suggests that it was recited during worship or funeral ceremonies.

Upon reading Professor Keskìn's descriptions, I was struck by memories of incantations I'd heard at the many funerals in the Eastern churches of Beirut, where I grew up. The church of my childhood conducted its ceremonial prayers and liturgy in two languages, alternating between Syriac and Arabic; however, when it came to prayers for the dead, the chants—rich in rhyme and repeated refrains—were recited only in Aramaic, a dying Semitic language. Today, remnants of this language, sometimes referred to as Syriac or as Western Neo-Aramaic, survive, barely, in a small Christian community in the embattled town of Maaloula, Syria.

During the years of the Lebanese Civil War, my family and I experienced a high frequency of deaths. The many funerals we attended inevitably inscribed these prayers in my memory, and these chants of death still occasionally resurface in my mind to this day. The fragments of prayers that survive in these fleeting languages, in the most unexpected places, become reminders both of ephemerality and the hermetically sealed words and history that are waiting to be revoked and rebirthed through academic and artistic encounters.

To return to Item III-200, the multiple languages that coexist in this fragment reflect the linguistic and religious diversity of the Turfan Basin, and a sequence of religious and cultural influences that accrued there over time. The languages of Turfan ranged from Middle Persian to Sogdian, from Parthian and Uyghur to Chinese, as well as Syriac, the ancestral language attributed to the Christians who reached that area. These communities lived a syncretic existence—a merging and assimilation of distinct traditions—and this intermingling is crucial to the exquisite and exalted quality of their writings and their religious paintings.

I was drawn to Item III-200, because it contains only words—no pictures, drawings or visual illuminations. I myself am a writer and a photographer, but in this instance I wished to set aside pictorial representation and focus on written practices. I was born not far from Byblos, Lebanon. Ancient Byblos is considered to be the place where the first alphabet was invented. The Phoenician alphabet, also called Early Linear Script, is the likely ancestor to the Greek and Latin alphabets.

Item III-200 has a dual nature. Its two sides contain writings in Old Uyghur, a Turkic language, and Sogdian, and they are written in two different colors, black and red. Nevertheless, the three hymns, eloquently described by Professor Keskìn as poems, belong to the same Manichaean belief system. These hymns share the same piece of paper, the same physicality, a duality within a unity. The body of this piece of paper is reminiscent of an argument within the Christian church with regard to Christ's incarnate being: *monos* (only divine) or *duos* (divine and human). Indeed, the Nestorians, persecuted as heretics, took refuge in the Turfan region between the seventh and eleventh centuries; they believed that Christ had a dual nature, that the divine and human coexisted in his being. The Nestorians, while integrating into the many languages of the Turfan region, continued to use Syriac as the language for religious matters.

Item III-200 is a fragment pertaining to Manichaean ceremonial practices. In other words, these papers are the remains of a religion that no longer exists, yet what remains in our hands today is a prayer for the dead, a sort of a requiem to itself, a chanting troubadour displaced from its original home, resurfacing to tell its own history.

On Manichaeism

Manichaeism was founded by the prophet Mani, born in 216 CE in the city of Mardinu, in the Parthian Empire, in the region of Babylonia. He wrote seven scriptures, the majority of which were in Aramaic, and his doctrine was intended to bring the many religions of his time together. Manichaeism belongs to the branch of Gnostic religions that includes some sects of Islam, mainly the Sufi order, and many branches of early Christianity. Gnosticism, from the Greek *gnōstikos*—"knowing, able to discern, good at knowing"—holds that illumination is a form of secret knowledge. Salvation or enlightenment can only be attained by acquiring certain learnings and by practicing a specific way of living. In contrast to the idea of revelation, which may be more accessible to the common believer through an available scripture, the Gnostic knowledge towards salvation is retained by a strata of knowers, people chosen to receive the knowledge, and transmitted within that select group.

My interest in the Manichaean religion come through my Christian education as a child. In reading *The Confession of St. Augustine*, I learned that the Father of Catholicism abandoned his forefathers' religion, Manichaeism, to embrace Christianity. This first exposure to a heretical religion intrigued me as a young man. And, eventually, it led me to another quest towards past forgotten religions.

The literature of Manichaeism is full of lamentation, forlornness and dread—homesickness for a higher realm, for a sun God who was lost, for a home of light to which we mortals, prisoners of this inferior existence, seek to return. In the beginning, the Manichaean mythology tells us, there was a world of light and a world of darkness, unknown to one another. Darkness was divided against itself, engaged in an internal warfare in which its members fought and devoured one another. Then they caught sight of the light. They marveled at it and longed to mix with it, possess it, and bring it into their power. Upon seeing this, the God of Light sent an army led by his son to fight inside the world of darkness. Unfortunately for the God of Light, the army of the Son of Light was defeated, fragmented and devoured. Entrapped, these scattered pieces of light lost their origins.

In the Manichaean belief system, each of us contains these splinters of light. The only way for us to return to our original home is through knowledge. This knowledge comes to us from celestials in the world of light who send us, their exiled relatives, "the call." A Gnostic Mandaean text, the "Hymn of the Pearl," describes "the call" this way:

> At the sound of his voice, I woke and arose from my slumber ... and directed my steps [so] that I might come to the light of our home.

The hymns in surviving Manichaean texts are lamentations protesting our confinement in this inferior world, this abode of captivity; we seek out the call that might return us to our original place of belonging.

Humans have the same fate as, for example, an object we are endeavoring to repatriate to a lost home. The ideas carried by Gnosticism and its predecessors, including Zoroastrianism, arise in many later religions, literatures and poetry. Gnostic doctrines of entrapment, liberation and return—of discontent with this existence, and return or restitution to the place of origin—encapsulate ideas found within many major religious and philosophical movements. We find its subtle traces in the *Rubaiyat* of Omar Khayyam and the philosophy of Friedrich Nietzsche. Omar Khayyam voices this protest against exile:

> There was a door to which I found no key
> there was a veil through which I might not see

The Syrian poet Abu al-Ala al-Ma'arri, a ninth-century atheist and antinatalist, rebels against this condemned existence:

> This crime [of birth] my father committed against me, while I have never committed this crime against anyone.

In the seventeenth century, Blaise Pascal writes of how he has been "engulfed in the infinite immensity of spaces of which I am ignorant, and which know me not, I am frightened, and am astonished at being here rather than there." Two hundred years later, in *Thus Spoke Zarathustra*, Nietzsche laments, "Woe unto him who has no home!" Closer to our own time, Martin Heidegger explores the state of *Geworfenheit*, "having been thrown into the world."

These lines, I must admit, shaped my novelistic writings. I have, in my own preferences towards an existentialist literary work, written with these philosophical, theological convictions in mind. And I became convinced that all novelistic work ought to have the same concern, to write against the attained answer, to engage with the magnitude of an unsolved question, the tragedy of existence.

Before its disappearance beneath the layers of other philosophies and religions, Manichaeans, perhaps uniquely among the Gnostics, believed salvation to be available to all. Mani's doctrine was intended to bring all the religions of his time together; he acknowledged all previous prophets and messengers and sought universality. A Manichaean's purpose was to free the light trapped in the material world so that it could rise to a paradise made of light. For nearly a hundred years in the ninth century, Manichaeism was the state religion of the Uyghur Kingdom in the Turfan region. Sometime in the fourteenth century, however, in the wake of various wars and persecutions, Manichaeism disappeared. Its scriptures are preserved in a fragmentary nature, in different languages.

Item III-200, therefore—these three hymns in Old Uyghur and Sogdian, with their prayers for the dead, their requiem—contains fragments of light that are still mixed with our world. One wonders to what world they can return, and to whom they call.

What Is a Thing?

In the Christian nativity story, three kings come from Persia bearing gifts. We know almost nothing about these men, only that they were members of the priestly order, or Magi. However, the objects they carried—gold, frankincense and myrrh—are known. Christianity, despite emphasizing the immateriality of our world, needed objects to celebrate the arrival of the child Jesus. They set a gift-giving precedent, inadvertently connecting Christianity to the material world. Throughout human history, objects have metamorphosed from mere existing things into religious offerings, instantly elevating themselves to the sacred: things made by the gods which transform into gifts to the gods. The slaughter of animals by the ancient Greeks turned livestock into sacrificial objects for the appeasement of deities. The elevation of a black stone to a place of pilgrimage in Islam is also a transformation of a natural material into a sacred one.

But, actually, what is an object? To quote Martin Heidegger:

> From the range of the fundamental questions of metaphysics, we shall ask this question: What is a thing? The question is quite old. What remains new about it is that the question must be asked repeatedly.[1]

I think the life of an object is a deeply involuted existence. A stone or a warrior's sword or the statue of a cat can be elevated from its worldly function to a transcendental status. The symbolic potentiality of any object is intrinsic and is drawn forth by the mutability of our projections, narratives, representations and intentions. We use objects to assert status, to accompany the dead when they are buried, as survival tools, as political tools, as objects of devotion and even corruption.

In my youth, during the war, my father owned a gun. He had no intention of using it—nor, I believe, did he have the capacity or knowledge needed to use a gun—but I recall that he maintained this weapon as an object of status among other collectors of guns. Guns suddenly took on, if I may project, a material status, a retreat from an object of war to an object of passive admiration for what the philosopher Walter Benjamin refers to as a passionate collector, and that collector represents a special form of preserving history, a concept of historical materialism.[2]

With each object we elevate, there is a story. Some objects that we revere were made by enslaved people, by child labor, by obscure craftspeople; if we take into account all of history, most masterpieces were fabricated by artists whose names will never be known.

When it comes to conquests, pillaging and thievery, as well as study and research that has the potential to illuminate, objects are clearly never neutral.

This idea brings us to this edifice, the Humboldt Forum, its collections and its narratives, which writers have been invited to contest. What precisely do you hope we will contest? Are we objecting to the practices of Western colonialism which created an unprecedented system of object acquisition, commodification, classification and transfer? Are we, as guests, supposed to remind you of your destructions and your ephemerality? Or are we here to discuss how the things we as a culture claim to preserve are also what we most want to conceal?

On Iconoclasm

Item III-200 was unearthed in the Turfan region,[3] a place of high mountains and deep valleys where numerous religions arrived and disappeared, only to be reborn again in various forms. As in many other places, forms of iconoclasm contributed, over the centuries, to the vandalism of some images and faces and the destruction of some manuscripts.[4] Lilla Russell-Smith notes that Item III-200, alongside a small collection of Manichaean fragments, was saved from decay and disappearance, from rain or snow, from agricultural activity and from human destruction by the German Turfan expeditions;[5] these fragments, as pieces of original Manichaean texts, are rare and precious, as they "came from Manichaeans themselves and not, as was the case with most of the texts known up to then, from the bitter enemies of this religion.[6]

That said, allow me to step away, for a moment, from Item III-200 and reflect on histories of destruction and rescue, which are part of the larger context of the Humboldt Forum. I would like to think about these questions via the Manichaean philosophy to which it belongs.

In our era, we have witnessed the destruction of the two-thousand-year-old Temple of Baalshamin in Palmyra, Syria, by the self-proclaimed Islamic State in 2015; a year earlier, they took sledgehammers to ancient objects in the Mosul Museum in Iraq and broke them into tiny fragments. Of course, iconoclasm is not practiced solely by the Islamic State, and such incidents occurred in Christian Europe. The mob attack on the Antwerp cathedral on August 20, 1566, is just one of many examples of the sixteenth-century Iconoclastic Fury. Early Christians attacked the statues of Hellenic figures around the Acropolis, to the future dismay of Nietzsche, who was fond of pronouncing his love for Hellenic antiquity.

We tend to think that iconoclasm is something archaic and of the past. Permit me to wonder, however, if our own capitalist society has created a new iconoclasm: a modern and secular kind. Let me explain. Historical objects have become the products that our capitalist society most carefully preserves, archives, classifies and, indeed, makes immobile. In short, such precious objects are hidden and shelved. We claim that we wish to preserve them forever, save them from the decay of existence and lead them to a future time.

The sheer amassing of objects in Europe over the last two centuries has made it impossible to display all that is contained in these collections—despite Europe's many museums, arts institutions and palatial buildings. In this capitalist society, where everything is consumed or traded, exchanged, relocated, bought and sold and conspicuously displayed, historical objects have fallen into another realm. They are either briefly displayed or preserved in massive warehouses. My criticism here is in no way meant to diminish the act of preservation, which is essential to the preservation of knowledge; I lament that our systems of education do not integrate tangled histories more fully into the curriculum.

I picture dusty warehouses filled with cabinets. I picture wooden boxes reminiscent of buried caves of worship waiting to be excavated and revealed, or relocated to oblivion.

These historical objects have become some of the most cloistered and stacked materials: a modern variation of iconoclasm. These objects can be displayed but never seen in completion—only in fragments. Indeed, some were violently fragmented when displaced from their original environment. They have become once more the victims of the sledge-hammer and the knife of this capitalist iconoclasm.

Expulsion

Researching Item III-200, I found myself watching a short documentary on the excavation, study and digitization of Turfan's Bezeklik Cave 15. In horror, I watched a re-enactment of a hand using a knife to slice through the magnificent wall paintings, the frescos found in Buddhist and Manichaean sanctuary caves. The arrival of archaeologists,[7] adventurers and treasure hunters,[8] from Germany, England, Russia, Japan, the United States and other nations to these caves beginning in the early 1900s, in order to slice off pieces[9] and carry them away, was, for me, chilling. The brutality of seeing a knife slicing through the gathered colors of the deities and worshippers portrayed on these sacred, hidden walls was like witnessing the expulsion of a thousand artisans and the scattering of their gods.

The Return

What I am intrigued about, concerning our topic of restitution, is the notion of return—a return to a place of origin; a return, according to Manichaeans, to the original light. Are our objects longing to return? Are objects capable of such a return? And what is the new knowledge we are expecting from these objects' salvation and liberation from entrapment?

For the Turfan region and the Bezeklik caves, the Manichaean mythology of dispersal and longing for return is embedded in the nature of the objects. Therefore, the fate of Item III-200 is part of that mythology. If, today, that particular item were to be returned, would it go to China, to the Uyghur communities in the Xinjiang Autonomous Region who are currently living under horrific oppression, or to Mani's place of birth in present-day Iraq? Is it too splintered, too rare, too fragile to make yet another journey?[10] Does the God of Light still exist to host these objects back in their original home? And if it does, is the light dormant in its being, immobile, unpolluted, unchanged?

In Manichaeism, the doctrine of mixing and unmixing sits at the heart of its cosmological system; its story of dispersal is closely related to an unwanted mixing—the slicing of the army of the Son of Light and the devouring, by our inferior world, of its luminosity, beauty and unity. In the Bezeklik caves, masterpieces of light and devotion were cut away and dispersed throughout a foreign, and perhaps uncomprehending, world. What befell Manichaeism through its dispersal was, inadvertently, the potential for a universal belonging, a sort of hybridity. These splinters of light dispersed throughout creation: One may hope and imagine that these splinters shone some light in their darkest places of confinement.

I suggest an unorthodox solution for the problem of return. As an artist whose calling is to imagine,

I am aware of the bureaucratic challenges of what I am proposing. Regardless, I propose it anyway. I call for an autonomous Republic of Objects. Museums all over the world would turn into places of refuge, where all objects are no longer the possessions of nations, private collectors or state institutions, but are under the care of an international body of librarians. The task of the librarians will be to return that which is possible to be returned and care for and share that which has no home. I believe that libraries, with their egalitarian public access, could become a great means for the diffusion and visibility of these objects for communities on a local level.

I know that not all are capable of returning. Having myself experienced a long civil war, the loss of a home and the impossibility of return, I feel a certain ambiguity with regard to the fate of the dispersed, this rupture which brings devastating loss and the wonder of experiencing the elsewhere which is part of survival. There is an impossibility of return, and of perfect justice and retribution, that every exile or refugee must eventually face because the original home has itself departed. The homes of childhood, the vision of light, the longing for a past—one eventually faces their passage. Do some objects feel the same, one might ask? Was the intention of the Manichaean gods and their light to be cut and fragmented, thrown into this world, dispersed and mixed? To be imperfectly seen yet known by both ignorance and knowledge, so that they could be reborn again and thus remain?

And yet our history is also full of successful returns, despite adversity. From Odysseus to men and women of the present, they have, at times, returned to a dimmer light, a changed paradise. They made the journey back regardless of the hardship and the consequences of arrival.

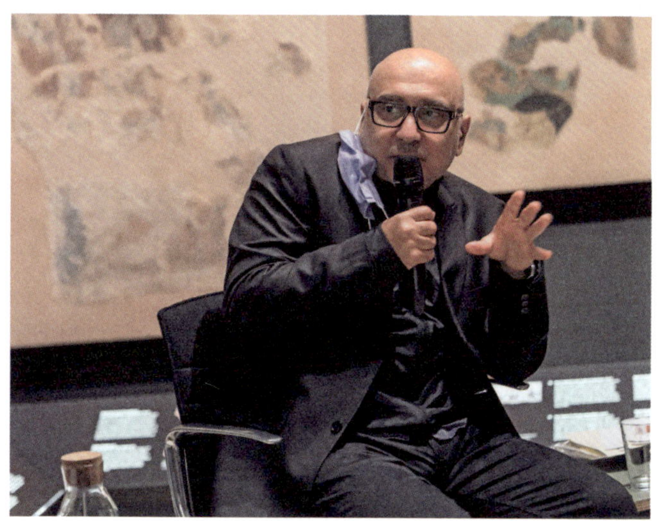

Rawi Hage at the Humboldt Forum

Notes

1 Martin Heidegger, *The Question Concerning the Thing*, trans. James D. Reid and Benjamin D. Crowe (Lanham, Maryland: Rowman and Littlefield International, 2018). | **2** Walter Benjamin, *Unpacking My Library: A Talk about Collecting* (London: Penguin Books, 2025). | **3** Specifically, Item III-200 is part of a collection of Manichaean fragments, rare and extremely precious, located in a site known as Ruin K in Kocho: "Once one of the most important cities of the eastern Tarim basin, Kocho has been the object of several explorations, starting from the end of the 19th century… followed by systematic archaeological investigation carried out by Albert Grünwedel and Albert von Le Coq between 1902 [and] 1914 (the so-called German Turfan Expeditions), and by Aurel Stein ([between] 1907 and 1914–1915). As is well known, the most significant documentation, and one which scholars are still relying on for their research, is that collected by the German expeditions, now kept at the Museum für Asiatische Kunst in Berlin." Yoko Nishimura, Erika Forte and Asanobu Kitamoto, "A New Method for Re-Identifying Ancient Excavated Structures on the Silk Road — The Case of Kocho," *The Ruins of Kocho: Traces of Wooden Architecture on the Ancient Silk Road*, ed. Lilla Russell-Smith and Ines Konczak-Nagel (Berlin: Museum für Asiatische Kunst, 2016), p. 59. | **4** "Most Manichaean fragments were found in… the so-called Library Room of Ruin K, [including] III-200. These tiny bits of paper would have been definitely destroyed by the 1980s by lack of interest, by rain/snow and by agricultural activity … Le Coq speaks of locals throwing cartloads of manuscripts into the river (because they thought of them as books from the devil). Whether true or not these leaves would have disappeared without the expeditions … If any deliberate destruction took place that was by the locals, [e.g.,] Buddhists. The so-called library in Ruin K (as quoted above) showed that the temple there was used by Manichaeans then Buddhists then Manichaeans again, and this change was not peaceful." Lilla Russell-Smith, email to the author, September 29, 2023. | **5** "This page was rescued and not destroyed, all Manichaean scriptures were rescued and not destroyed by the Germans." Lilla Russell-Smith, email to the author. | **6** "F. W. K. Müller discovered in the first texts sent to Berlin not only Middle Iranian languages but also original Manichaean texts. Texts thereby came to light that were from Manichaeans themselves and not, as was the case with most of the texts known up to then, from the bitter enemies of this religion or from slightly more objective Arabic historians, and therefore opened a new door on Manichaeism. Work on them has given new impulses to the study of Manichaeism and Gnosis. Later discoveries of Manichaean and Gnostic texts—especially in Greek and Coptic—have led to a more profound understanding of the texts of Eastern Manichaeism and allowed their relative position to be established." Berlin-Brandenburg Academy of Sciences and Humanities, *Turfan Studies* (2007), p. 18. | **7** "I have worked since the 1990s with the meticulous correspondence of (Sir) Aurel Stein, who died in Kabul, where it was his dream to see Gandharan art, but he caught pneumonia there in his 80s, and died and was buried there. Although born into a Hungarian Jewish family and educated partly in Germany, he went to British India and later became a British citizen. You could call him a Euro-centric finding the traces of Antique culture so far East. He was a brilliant linguist. Stein photographed and described everything meticulously—we catalogued his photographs and papers left to the Hungarian Academy of Sciences. You could call him colonial. But not an adventurer." Lilla Russell-Smith, email to the author, October 2, 2023. | **8** "The fiasco [of the failed Fogg expedition to Dunhuang] of 1925 did not faze [Harvard art historian Langdon] Warner in the least bit. Over the next five years, the chronic political instability of China apparently convinced Warner and other explorers who followed in his wake that it would still be possible to take first and ask later." Justin M. Jacobs, *The Compensations of Plunder: How China Lost Its Treasures* (Chicago: University of Chicago Press, 2020), p. 203. | **9** "[W]hen [Aurel] Stein and Pelliot first witnessed the excavation methods of German archaeologists Le Coq and Grünwedel in Kucha, Turfan, and Karashahr, they could scarcely believe their eyes. Pelliot was the first to see the indelicate handiwork of the Germans, who 'made "holes" and conducted themselves more in "Sarte," seeking objects for their museums more than working for science.' The following year, Pelliot concluded that the

Germans 'have completely ruined the Ming-oi' at Kara-shahr by hacking at the frescos and putting 'strong glue in the hollow inscriptions; why great gods?' Stein, a far more guarded commentator than Pelliot, also found it difficult to reserve judgment on the Germans. Like Pelliot, however, he would only criticize the Germans in private. 'You will understand the awkward dilemma I had to face,' he wrote to his good friend Percy Allen from Ming-oi in December 1907, 'when I found ruin after ruin of big temples, monasteries etc., dug into with the method of a scholarly treasure seeker, yet barely explored with any approach to archaeological thoroughness.' After repeatedly encountering seemingly deliberate gashes to murals the Germans left behind, along with a general 'indifference to the fate of all that was left in situ,' Stein described Le Coq's excavation methods as a 'system for which the German language supplies the express term of Rabbau.' The passage of time did not lessen Stein's distaste for German depredations. 'It has needed practice to examine calmly the way in which Lecoq's & Grunwedel's assistant,' Stein observed on his third expedition in 1915, 'had ruthlessly hacked the frescoes to the right & left of the pieces they wanted.' The Russian explorer Sergey Oldenburg was far more blunt. 'It is sheer robbery, clever, ingenious, but robbery all the same—not scholarly research.'" Jacobs, *Compensations of Plunder*, pp. 42–43. | **10** "In fact I wish there were more Manichaean objects. I have had to turn down so many institutions borrowing fragments, as there is really only a handful in good condition, and during COVID and the other upheavals of recent times I have become very aware of how fragile they all are. They would fit into a small box, and if I were to loan this small box to another museum, Manichaean manuscripts from the Turfan Region could disappear in flames, be destroyed in water, or in an earthquake or whatever disasters may happen.... This fragility and the miracle of how these pages still contain so much are the main message for me in your text." Lilla Russell-Smith, email to the author, September 29, 2023.

OBJECTS
TALK BACK

Priya Basil
Locked In and Out

Preface by Hartmut Dorgerloh

Few buildings are as controversial as the new Berlin Palace, which now houses the Humboldt Forum. In Germany and beyond, people wonder why an imperial palace was rebuilt in the centre of Berlin and then filled with the often violently acquired ethnological collections of the Prussian Cultural Heritage Foundation. The writer Priya Basil unfurls the story of the palace reconstruction alongside a personal story of her migrating to Berlin. She questions what such a building means for our understanding of the past and our sense of belonging in the present. "In German the word Schloss means a palace, and also a 'lock.' The central question: Can a lock also be a key?"

Meena Kandasamy
A Wise One, a Warrior

Preface by Priya Basil

The Mithuna couple is a 17th-century ivory sculpture from Tamil Nadu (India) depicting lovers. Meena Kandasamy examines how caste and class are carved into the object as indelibly as its physical details. She unfurls worlds of possibility around this seemingly idyllic couple, connecting them to personal and political stories that expose painful realities of who gets to love whom. With astonishing narrative flair—mixing X threads, academic discourse, poetry, memoir—she lets the object talk and talk back.

OBJECTS
TALK BACK

Léonora Miano
Ladies of the Throne

Preface by Priya Basil

"Most of the time, it is the power of men that we remember." These words open Léonora Miano's narrative about Mandu Yenu, a throne from the ancient Kingdom of Bamum (present-day Cameroon). The Germans long claimed the object was a "gift" from King Njoya to Kaiser Wilhelm II. Miano reads "between the lines of beads and cowrie shells" to show the complexity of colonial and gender relations. She reveals that Mandu and Yenu were royal wives in the Kingdom of Bamum. The very name of the object suggests it—it is the power of women that we should remember.

Madeleine Thien
The Artisans

Preface by Priya Basil

Canadian writer Madeleine Thien reflects on a fragment of a mural depicting three Uyghur princes from one of the Bezeklik Caves along the Northern Silk Road, in what is now the Xinjiang Uyghur Autonomous Region of China. This most renowned donor portrait of Uyghur-Buddhist art was brought to the Berlin museums following the Second German Turfan Expedition (1904–1905). Thien responds to its vibrant colors and expressive lines with a fictional text, transporting us into the daily lives of the painters who adorned the caves with strikingly lifelike murals in the tenth century. She asks: Is there an autonomous republic of art that transcends time and place?

Published by Stiftung Humboldt Forum im Berliner Schloss

Concept: Priya Basil
Project management: Katharina Kepplinger
Text editing: James Copeland
Image editing: Barbara Martinkat

Special thanks to Fränze Czaja, Han Song Hiltmann and Jan Linders (SHF) as well as to Lilla Russell-Smith (SMB) for their friendly support.

www.humboldtforum.org

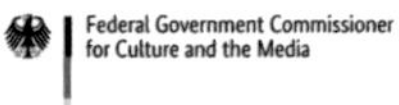

Funded by the Federal Government Commissioner for Culture and the Media in line with a resolution by the German Federal Parliament

External links contained in the text could be reviewed only up to the publication date. The issuer and publisher have had no influence on later changes and can therefore accept no liability. The Deutsche Nationalbibliothek lists this publication in the Deutsche Nationalbibliografie; detailed bibliographic data are available on the Internet at http://dnb.dnb.de.

ISBN 978-3-0358-0795-0
Layout: 2edit, Zurich
Printed in Germany

DIAPHANES – Schöneggstrasse 5 – CH-8004 Zurich
DIAPHANES Berlin – Dresdener Strasse 118 – 10999 Berlin – kontakt@diaphanes.net